3 5000 09538 8582

W9-AYO-196

Blake Griffin

SUPERSTARS IN THE WORLD OF BASKETBALL

LeBron James

Dwyane Wade

Kobe Bryant

Carmelo Anthony

Kevin Durant

Chris Paul

Dwight Howard

Rajon Rondo

Blake Griffin

Players & the Game Around the World

SUPERSTARS IN THE WORLD OF BASKETBALL

Blake Griffin

Shaina Indovino

Mason Crest

Mason Crest
450 Parkway Drive, Suite D
Broomall, PA 19008
www.masoncrest.com

Printed and bound in the United States of America.

First printing
9 8 7 6 5 4 3 2 1

Series ISBN: 978-1-4222-3101-2
ISBN: 978-1-4222-3102-9
ebook ISBN: 978-1-4222-8792-7

Cataloging-in-Publication Data on file with the Library of Congress.

Contents

KEY ICONS TO LOOK FOR:

Text-Dependent Questions: These questions send the reader back to the text for more careful attention to the evidence presented there.

Words to Understand: These words with their easy-to-understand definitions will increase the reader's understanding of the text, while building vocabulary skills.

Series Glossary of Key Terms: This back-of-the book glossary contains terminology used throughout this series. Words found here increase the reader's ability to read and comprehend higher-level books and articles in this field.

Research Projects: Readers are pointed toward areas of further inquiry connected to each chapter. Suggestions are provided for projects that encourage deeper research and analysis.

Sidebars: This boxed material within the main text allows readers to build knowledge, gain insights, explore possibilities, and broaden their perspectives by weaving together additional information to provide realistic and holistic perspectives.

Words to Understand

opponents: Players on the other team.
dominating: Controlling with skill.
standardized: All the same or equal. Standardized tests measure how well different children from different places do on the same test.
draft: The way NBA teams pick players from college or high school teams to join the league.

Starting Out

The clock is ticking, and Blake has to act fast. He has no time to think and needs to trust his instincts. His teammate, Kobe Bryant, is dribbling the ball down the court. Kobe gets closer to the basket, but some of his ***opponents*** block him. He won't be able to shoot and score because his shot will be blocked. Now is Blake's chance. He sprints toward the basket and jumps high into the air.

Without Blake saying a word, Kobe knows what to do. He passes the ball to Blake, who slams it into the hoop. The crowd goes wild. Blake swings on the hoop for a moment before he drops to the floor and gets ready for his next play. The other team already has the ball, and he'll have to work with his teammates if he wants to win this game.

Blake Griffin and Kobe Bryant are playing for the West team in the 2013 All-Star Game. Their teammates are some of the best players in the NBA. Together, they are ***dominating*** the court. Blake scores dunk after dunk, something he is famous for. His other teammates catch rebounds, block shots, and shoot amazing three-point shots from across the court. The buzzer finally sounds, and the West Team is declared the winner.

Blake grew up in Oklahoma City, where he was homeschooled and then went to high school in the city. Blake learned his love of basketball in his home city and didn't leave until he headed to college.

Make Connections

All basketball players have strengths and weaknesses. Blake Griffin is best known for his ability to dunk. A dunk occurs when a basketball player runs up to the basket, jumps up, and pushes the ball through the hoop. Dunking is hard to do in the NBA because the basket is ten feet above the ground. Blake has to jump very high after pushing past his opponents to successfully dunk the ball.

It takes many basketball players years of practice to make it to the All-Star Game. Blake is an exception. He has played in the NBA for only three years, but he is no stranger to All-Star games. Blake was first asked to join the West All-Star Team as a rookie in 2010. He has gone to every All-Star Game since then.

Getting to Blake Griffin's level of talent takes many years of hard work. Like many athletes, Blake started playing basketball when he was still young. Both his parents and his brother pushed him to keep improving himself both on the court and off. His father, who is a basketball coach, guided Blake to become the great player he is today. For Blake, the sky is the limit. He hopes to win a championship, compete in the Olympics, and even join the Hall of Fame by the end of his career.

BLAKE AND TAYLOR

Blake Austin Griffin was born on March 16, 1989, in Oklahoma City, Oklahoma. He has one brother, Taylor, who is three years older than him. Blake and Taylor's father, Tommy, is African American, while their mother, Gail, is white. Blake looked up to Taylor in every way while they were growing up. The two brothers played sports together from an early age. Some of the sports they played included basketball, baseball, and football.

Tommy and Gail supported Blake and Taylor's desire to be athletes. Tommy played basketball and was a member of the track team when he was in high school. His dedication to sports did not end when he graduated. Tommy found a way to continue his passion even as an adult. He owns a company that makes trophies to award athletes on a job well done. Tommy is also the basketball coach of a team in Oklahoma City.

Gail worked as a teacher both before and after her children were born. She planned to keep teaching, but all of that changed when Blake entered daycare. Tommy and Gail sent their children to daycare so that they could both go to work during the day.

Taylor had had no problem adjusting to life in a daycare—but Blake did not like it. He would cry every time his parents tried to take him there. Seeing her son cry like that broke Gail's heart. She didn't want to leave him alone at daycare if he didn't want to be there.

Many families decide to homeschool their children instead of sending them to school with other kids. Blake and Taylor were both taught by their mother Gail for years when they were younger. For the Griffins, homeschooling was the right choice, but each family makes their own choices about homeschool.

Make Connections

Trophies and other awards have been around for thousands of years. In ancient Greece, the winners of the Olympic games received wreaths made out of laurel leaves. Later, the winner also received a tall jar filled with sacred olive oil. In other ancient games, winners received silver cups or chalices filled with wine or oil. Over the years, winners no longer received the wine and oil—but they still were awarded cup-shared trophies. Today, trophies are much less expensive, thanks to mass-produced plastic trophies, and even young athletes receive them.

Gail decided to quit her job and stay home with her boys. When they were old enough to go to school, she continued to teach them at home. She was an experienced teacher, and she enjoyed homeschooling Taylor and Blake.

Learning at home is very different from going to a public school. Instead of attending classes, Taylor and Blake were taught by their mother at the dining room table. Children who are homeschooled are taught the same material children in school must learn. All children are tested on the material each year through ***standardized*** tests. Subjects that are tested include math, geography, history, and English. All children must pass these tests to move on to the next grade.

Gail taught her children more than enough to pass the tests each year, but she also included a few lessons of her own. She believed that it was important to teach her children about religion and God. Taylor and Blake were homeschooled until Blake was in eighth grade and Taylor was in tenth.

Blake and Taylor each always wanted to be the first to complete an assignment, and they turned everything into a competition. Everything they did became a race between the two brothers, from sports to homework.

Like many young brothers, Blake and Taylor also fought a lot. Gail broke up the fights by sending Blake and Taylor to opposite areas of the house. This helped them cool off. Although they fought a lot, Blake and Taylor were both great brothers and good friends. They went almost everywhere together and continued playing sports with each other up until they entered the NBA draft in 2009.

TEAM SPORTS

Homeschooled children don't have opportunities to make friends at school, so Taylor and Blake's parents made sure they had chances to interact with kids their age by entering them in various team sports. Their teammates soon became their friends.

Basketball was Blake's favorite sport as a child, but soon, the sport would become much more than a hobby.

Today, Blake's childhood friend Sam Bradford plays quarterback for the St. Louis Rams. Here, Bradford, number 8, is about to throw a pass during a game against the San Francisco 49ers.

Blake and Taylor did not limit themselves to just one sport while they were growing up. They played football, baseball, and basketball in a youth league. Blake played as a first baseman in baseball and a wide receiver in football. It wasn't until high school that Blake picked his favorite sport and dedicated all of his time to it.

One of Blake's closest friends growing up was Sam Bradford. Sam was a great football player who went on to become the top pick in the 2010 NFL ***draft***. Sam's family owned a local gym named the Bradford Complex. Taylor, Blake, and Sam would spend hours playing together at the gym. Taylor and Blake loved to practice various sports on their driveway at home, as well.

Basketball quickly became Blake's favorite sport, but he did have one problem. Basketball players are usually very tall and muscular. They need to be big and strong in order to run down the court, pass the ball to teammates, and make amazing shots when they are far away from the basket. Blake eventually grew up to be six feet and ten inches tall, but to his childhood friends, he was known as "Little Griffin," a nickname he didn't like. Because of their age difference, Taylor was always much bigger than Blake while they were growing up. Blake needed to work long and hard if he ever wanted to be as good at sports as his older brother. He did a lot to keep himself in shape and running was a huge part of his training. The drive to make himself better helped Blake become the successful basketball star he is today.

Tommy and Gail Griffin are another part of why their sons became such successful athletes. They pushed Blake and Taylor to get better at sports, but they also asked them to work hard at home. Blake and Taylor had lots of chores, like washing the dishes or taking out the trash. Sometimes, Blake and Taylor would help out with the family business. Blake said later, "My parents did most of the work, but we all had to help out." Like everything else, Blake and Taylor would race to see who could get done with their chores first.

HIGH SCHOOL

Blake and Taylor began high school at the Oklahoma Christian School in 2003. One of the reasons they chose this school was because their father was the head coach of the basketball team. Tommy had been helping their sons play basketball since they were first practicing hoops on the family driveway. By the time they reached high school, they were the star members of the team.

The Oklahoma Christian School basketball team did very well the year Blake joined. The Saints didn't lose a single game during the 2003–2004 season, and they went to the Class 3A boys' state championship. The Saints won the game 55 to 50. This year was only the beginning for Blake and his team. More championship victories were on the way.

The 2004–2005 season was almost as good as the year before. The Saints did not play a perfect season, but they came close. The Griffin brothers and their teammates won twenty-four games and lost only two that year. The Saints went to the championship again and did not come home empty-handed. The Oklahoma Christian School won the game with 51 points. The opposing team only had 34.

Blake really began to shine during the 2004–2005 season. He averaged about 13 points per game. Blake scored 12 points and 9 rebounds in the state championship game.

Research Project

A sidebar in this chapter tells a little about the history of trophies. Using the library and the Internet, find out more about awards that were given to the winners of ancient games, starting with Greeks and Romans and continuing up through the Middle Ages in Europe. Explain how these early awards changed into our modern-day trophies. Draw pictures to illustrate what these trophies and other awards looked like.

Text-Dependent Questions

1. According to this chapter, how is Blake Griffin different from most other basketball players?
2. Describe what Blake's education was like during his grade-school years.
3. How did Blake's parents help him become the athlete he is today?
4. In what ways were Blake and his brother competitive with each other?

Sports fans in the area started to notice him, which is one of the reasons Blake was named to the Little All-City All-State team. Blake was also a member of the Athletes First Amateur Athletic Union (AAU) team during the summer of 2005. He played against future NBA stars such as Kevin Durant and Ty Lawson.

But Blake was just getting started.

Words to Understand

scholarship: Money given to a student in need so he can afford to go to college.
honorary: Given as an award.
professional: Paid to play. A "professional team" is a team in the NBA rather than a team of friends playing for fun.

Gaining Experience

Blake and Taylor stopped playing on the same team when Taylor went on to college. He received a ***scholarship*** to play for the University of Oklahoma at the start of the 2005–2006 school year. This left Blake to soak up more of the spotlight in high school.

Blake took Taylor's place as the star of the team. The Saints went to the state championship again, this time playing as a Class 2A team. The team easily won, with a final score of 57 to 40. Blake was named the Most Valuable Player (MVP) of the state championship game.

Blake's junior year was his best year yet. He averaged 21 points, 12 rebounds, and almost 5 assists. His performance was so good that the state's largest newspaper, the *Oklahoman*, named him Player of the Year. Another important Oklahoma newspaper, the *Tulsa World*, named him to its Boys All-State First Team.

Jeff Capel III (center) has had a long career in coaching college basketball, including at Duke and the University of Oklahoma. There, he coached both Blake and his brother Taylor.

Make Connections

Players who wanted to join the NBA were once able to declare for the NBA draft straight out of high school. In 2006, the rules of the NBA changed. Any athletes who wanted to declare for the NBA would have to wait until they were at least nineteen years old. This would give them a chance to improve and gain experience through a college team.

Blake needed to start thinking about his future now. He would need to go to college for at least one year before joining the NBA, and he had a lot of different schools to choose from.

Many people came to watch Blake play during his junior year, but the most important person was a man named Jeff Capel. Jeff was the head coach of the University of Oklahoma basketball team. He was also Taylor's coach. Jeff had first heard about Blake through Taylor, and Blake had practiced a few times with some of Taylor's teammates. It only took one game for Jeff to know that Blake was someone he wanted to bring onto the Oklahoma team.

Jeff asked Blake to join the Oklahoma Sooners, but Taylor was the one who convinced Blake to join the team. He told Blake that the Oklahoma Sooners would really be able to go somewhere if Blake was a part of the team. Blake also liked the idea of being able to play with his brother again, so he agreed to play for the University of Oklahoma. He made the decision just before the start of his senior year of high school.

Blake's final year with the Saints was great. His performance on the court was better than ever before. He averaged 26 points and 15 rebounds in the 2006–2007 season. Plenty of colleges were starting to notice Blake, including Duke, Kansas, North Carolina, and Texas. However, Blake had already chosen to join his brother at the University of Oklahoma. It was too late for all of the other schools!

Blake picked up many awards before he left high school. The *Oklahoman* named him Player of the Year again, and so did the *Tulsa World*. He was added to some ***honorary*** teams, including the Oklahoma Boys All-State First Team, the EA Sports All-American Second Team, and the *Parade* Third Team All-American.

The Saints won the state championship for a fourth year in a row, and Blake was named the MVP of the championship for a second year in a row. Blake was selected to play in a number of games, including the McDonald's All-American Game in Kentucky. One of the events during the game was a slam dunk contest. Blake easily won the contest. He showed the world a taste of what was to come once he entered college.

Football is a huge part of life at the University of Oklahoma. The Sooners have thousands of fans at the school and more all around the country.

Make Connections

The Big 12 Conference is a ten-school collegiate athletic conference headquartered in Irving, Texas. It is a member of the NCAA's Division I for all sports, including basketball and football. Colleges that are a part of the Big 12 are located in Iowa, Kansas, Oklahoma, Texas, and West Virginia. Blake set a lot of Big 12 records during his time with the University of Oklahoma. Some have not been broken.

COLLEGE

Blake knew he needed to spend at least one year in college to gain practice before he would be old enough to join the NBA. The Oklahoma Sooners were excited to have Blake join. The University of Oklahoma was best known for its football team before Blake started attending the school, but now, Blake helped to put the Oklahoma basketball team back on the map. Blake averaged about 14 points and 9 rebounds per game.

Basketball is a hard sport. Even athletes who are very careful can hurt themselves while playing the game they love. Blake is no different. He hurt himself a lot during his freshman year of college. He injured his left knee during one game, and his right knee a few weeks later. The second injury was so bad that Blake needed minor surgery to fix it, but he was back on the court within a week. Even with all of his injuries, Blake did well during his freshman year. He was named to the Big 12 All-Rookie Team.

Some people thought Blake would join the 2008 NBA draft now. Blake had proved he was good enough to play on a ***professional*** team, but he didn't want to leave the

Make Connections

There are five different positions on the basketball court. They are point guard, shooting guard, small forward, power forward, and center. Each position has a different role. Blake Griffin plays the position of power forward. Power forwards are offensive players. They get close to the basket and make a lot of close-range shots. Power forwards also grab a ball once it has rebounded off the rim or backboard. Some power forwards are great a making jump shots. Most power forwards in the NBA are very tall, with some reaching almost seven feet in height.

Blake leaps for the basket during a practice game the Clippers played for the Marines of Camp Pendelton and their families in 2009, Blake's first year in the NBA.

Research Project

Blake and Taylor Griffin played for the Sooners, the University of Oklahoma's team. Using the Internet, find out how the Sooners got their name and describe the history of this term.

Sooners just yet. He believed he would be able to take the Sooners all the way to a state title if he played with them for just one more year.

At first, it looked like Blake might be right. The 2008–2009 season started out well, with the Sooners having a streak of twelve wins. Blake had some great games. During one game, he scored 35 points and 21 rebounds alone. Scoring at least 10 points in two categories of basketball is known as a double-double. During his college career, Blake became known for his double-doubles and his ability to dunk.

Blake continued getting better and was rewarded for it by being named Player of the Week six times during his sophomore year. He beat own previous record when he scored 40 points and 23 rebounds in a single game. The Sooners finished the season with twenty-seven wins and five losses.

Blake and his teammates made it to the South Regional finals of the National College Athletic Association (NCAA) tournament. This was a huge improvement over past years, but the team did not get to celebrate for very long. The Sooners lost to the North Carolina Tar Heels and did not win the tournament like Blake had hoped they would.

By the end of Blake's sophomore year, he had scored at least 20 points and 15 rebounds in a game on fifteen separate occasions, becoming the first and only Big 12 athlete to do so. He also scored thirty double-doubles, just one shy of the NCAA record. Blake's total of 504 rebounds was also just one rebound short of a new record. In the 2008–2009 season, Blake won every single possible Player of the Year Award. There are six in total, and they are all awarded by a different organization.

Blake originally went to college to play with his brother and gain experience in a college basketball league. In just two years, he had achieved everything he wanted, and now he was ready to move on—so he joined the 2009 NBA draft. Many of Blake's fans and coaches believed he was ready now to become an NBA star.

NBA DRAFT

The NBA Draft takes place every year in June. The NBA teams with the worst record from the year before are allowed to pick new team members first. The draft is done this way so every team has a fair chance at doing well during the next season. If the best teams kept picking the best players, the other teams would not stand a chance in the playoffs.

Playing for the Clippers in Los Angeles would be a big change for Blake, a change that would include moving from his home state of Oklahoma to the California city.

Text-Dependent Questions

1. Explain the role that Jeff Capel played in Blake's life.
2. What does MVP stand for?
3. Explain how the NBA draft rules changed in 2006.
4. What is a double double?
5. What does a power forward do?

The players with the best record in high school or college will usually be chosen first in the draft. Blake's chances of being picked early on were very good. He was one of the best power forwards entering the draft that year. Many people expected Blake to be chosen early on—but they were surprised when Blake was the very first pick!

The Los Angeles Clippers were given the first choice, and they decided to take Blake onto their team as a strong power forward. The Clippers had not been doing so well, and they hoped Blake would turn the team around. Perhaps he would even be able to bring the team to a championship title one day!

Words to Understand

sophomores: Players in their second year.
contract: An agreement between at least two people or two groups of people.

Rookie of the Year

Joining the Los Angeles Clippers marked a very big change in Blake's life. He packed his bags, said goodbye to his family, and moved to the West Coast. It was the farthest he had ever been from his brother or his parents. Blake would miss his life in Oklahoma, but he was excited to finally be playing for an NBA team. He had worked for many years to get into the NBA, and now he was eager to show the world what he could do.

The official season doesn't begin until the fall, but Blake got an early start as a member of the Clippers' summer league. Blake's first few games as a Clipper went well. He scored impressive dunks during almost every game he played. He was even named the Summer League MVP because of his performance during those summer games. NBA fans all over the United States were excited to see what Blake would do during the regular season.

Playing for the Clippers was an amazing chance for Blake to play in front of millions of people and show his skills. In his first year with the team, the spotlight was on Blake like never before.

Make Connections

Each year, the NBA hosts an event for the best players in the NBA. One of the most popular events is the All-Star Game. Only the very best players in the NBA are chosen to play in the All-Star Game. Fans choose starters, while coaches choose the reserves. The teams are divided into East and West players. The All-Star game is usually one of the most intense games of the NBA season. Fans from all over the world watch the game on television.

BAD LUCK

Unfortunately, they didn't get the chance. Blake injured himself during the last game of the preseason. He hurt his left knee right after one of his famous slam dunks. He landed on his foot the wrong way and hurt his kneecap. X-rays showed that his kneecap was broken. Blake's doctors told him to rest for a few weeks to see if the injury would get better on its own.

Unfortunately, it did not. Blake would need surgery if he ever wanted to play basketball again. He finally had the operation in January of 2010, half a year after he joined the Clippers. After the surgery, his knee still needed to heal. He was unable to play for the rest of the year, which meant that he would not play a single game with the Clippers for the entire 2009–2010 season.

This was very hard on Blake. "I don't know what kind of word I'd used to describe it," Blake said later. "It was almost torture." Blake had waited many years to get his shot at playing for the NBA. He was chosen first in the 2009 NBA draft, but he hadn't played a single regular season game. Instead, he was forced to sit on the bench and watch his teammates have all the fun.

Blake wasn't the only one who was unhappy about his injury. His fans were disappointed, too. They had hoped Blake would bring the Clippers in a new direction. The Clippers did not do well without him, and they ended the 2009–2010 season with 53 losses.

Fortunately, Blake knew his knee would be healed by the start of his next season. He felt more than ready to finally show the Clippers and his fans what he could do for the team.

SECOND-YEAR ROOKIE

Players who are new to the NBA are called rookies. Rookies usually only keep this title for one year, but Blake's situation was different. He didn't get to play a single game during his first year, so he was still considered a rookie during his second year as a member of

The Clippers play at the Staples Center. The Los Angeles Lakers, WNBA team L.A. Sparks, and hockey team L.A. Kings also play at the arena.

the Clippers. His first official regular season game wasn't until the start of the 2010–2011 season.

Blake started the season with a bang. He became known for his dunks. His skills on the court were even greater than they'd been in college. In one game alone, he scored 44 points.

Even with Blake's help, however, the Clippers did not improve right away. The team lost all but one of the first eleven games of the season. Everything changed during the winter months, though.

Blake started attracting the attention of fans through his energetic plays. He was quick on his feet and fun to watch. Many of his fans went to watch him play at the Clipper's official stadium. He broke a record during one game when he won 47 points on his own in a game against the Indiana Pacers. One month later, Blake was selected as a reserve for the 2011 All-Star Game. Reserves do not play as often as other players during a game, but they are still very important. They play when the starters get tired or need a break.

Rookies are not usually chosen as members of the All-Star Team. The last time a rookie had been placed on the team before Blake Griffin was in 2003. Blake was placed on the West team because the Clippers are from the West Coast. The West team defeated the East team by only five points. Blake also played in a rookies-versus-***sophomores*** game where the rookies came out on top. One day before the All-Star Game, Blake also won the Sprite Slam Dunk Contest. Blake had a lot of reasons to be proud once he returned to the Los Angeles court.

In March, he added another reason to his list when he scored his first triple-double. A player scores a triple-double when he receives ten or more points in three separate categories in basketball. Blake recorded his first triple-double when he scored 39 points, 10 rebounds, and 10 assists in his final game of the 2010–2011 season.

Blake Griffin was a very special rookie, and the world knew it. He earned every single T-Mobile Rookie of the Month award that year, becoming the first player to do so since 2006. Blake blew away his fellow rookies in points, rebounds, and double doubles. He had more of these than any other rookie and even many of the older players. His averages were 22 points and 12 rebounds per game. He is only the twentieth first-year player in the history of the NBA to average at least 20 points and 10 rebounds per game. Blake was voted the tenth-best player in the NBA by ESPN in 2011—and he was only a rookie!

No one was surprised when Blake earned the Rookie of the Year award at the end of a very good year. The winner of this award is chosen by a group of sportswriters from all over the United States and Canada. Every single person who voted for the 2011 Rookie of the Year voted for Blake. Blake was the first unanimous winner of the award since 1990.

THE PLAYOFFS

By the start of the 2011–2012 season, everyone could see that Blake Griffin was one of the Clippers' most important players. But he couldn't turn the team around all by himself. The

The Staples Center, covered in advertisements for the 2011 All-Star Game, Blake's first. In 2011, the All-Star Game was held in Los Angeles, giving Blake the chance to play at his home arena.

team decided to pick up Chris Paul and Chauncey Billups, two experienced and talented NBA players the Clippers hoped would be enough to bring the team to victory. Blake, Chris, and Chauncey worked well together. They were able to bring the Clippers to the playoffs that year.

Blake was chosen to join the All-Star Game once more in 2012. This time, he would be a starter. Most sophomore players are not experienced enough to be a starter in the All-Star Game. Blake being chosen was a very special honor, and he did not disappoint his fans. He scored a total of 22 points and 5 rebounds in the game, helping the West team win by just 3 points.

A few months later, the Clippers qualified for the playoffs. NBA playoffs always happen after the regular season is over. The playoffs started out well for Blake and his teammates. The Los Angeles Clippers won the first round by defeating the Memphis Grizzlies in seven games. Blake was a huge part of the win. During one game, he scored 30 points all by himself. Several of those points were from his dazzling dunks. Unfortunately, the team lost in the next round against the San Antonio Spurs.

During the summer of 2012, Blake received a bigger honor than anything he had ever been given before. He was selected to join the United States national team, which would be going to London to compete in the 2012 Olympic Games. This was an opportunity Blake had always dreamed of, but he turned the offer down after he injured his knee again. Blake knew he needed to rest if he wanted to be ready for the 2012–2013 season with the Clippers. Maybe he would be able to join the Olympic Team next time, in 2016.

Blake renewed his ***contract*** with the Clippers at the start of the 2012–2013 season. He agreed to play for the team until the end of 2017–2018 season, which locked him in for another five years.

When Blake first joined the team as a rookie, he was not making a lot of money. Rookies usually do not. Young players need to prove themselves through many years of hard work before they are paid well. Blake had showed his worth on the court many times, though, and his new contract reflected that. He will earn a total of $95 million!

Blake was chosen as a member of the All-NBA Second Team in both 2012 and 2013. He also became an NBA All-Star for a third time that year. The West team won once

Research Project

According to this chapter, Blake Griffin will be earning $95 million as a basketball player. Using the Internet, compare Blake's salary to other basketball players'. What is the highest salary in the basketball world? Who earns it? Explain where the money for these salaries comes from.

Blake watches a 2011 game from the bench. Even when he couldn't play during the 2009-2010 season, Blake has always been there to support his team.

Text-Dependent Questions

1. Explain why Blake didn't get a chance to play during his first year in the NBA.
2. Define the term "rookie" as it is used in this chapter.
3. Explain how players are chosen for the All-Star Game.
4. What is a triple-double?

again with a lead of 5 points, and this made Blake a three-time NBA All-Star champion. He will likely be chosen for many more NBA All-Star games in the future.

The Clippers made it to the playoffs for a second year in a row during the 2012–2013 season. Just like the year before, Blake and his teammates were paired up against the Memphis Grizzlies in the first round. This time, the Grizzlies came out victorious when the team beat the Clippers in six games. Blake went home empty-handed, but he was filled with hope for the next year.

Words to Understand

donates: Gives (often money, food, or clothing).
charity: Groups who work to help others in need using money that people give the group.

Just the Beginning

Blake Griffin is still very young. He has many years left on the court. As of 2014, he had only played professionally for three seasons. (The 2009–2010 season does not count because he wasn't able to play a single game during the regular season.) Many players stay in the league for ten seasons or more. A rising basketball star like Blake Griffin has a lot of options.

Blake Griffin has never played in an international game. Many of his fans hope he will join the 2016 Olympic team, but that is not Blake's number-one goal. He wants to snag an NBA championship before anything else. After that, he can work on becoming an NBA Hall of Famer. Many other Clippers have the same goal. Blake hopes to lead the Clippers to victory in the NBA Finals one day.

Unfortunately, he can't do it alone. Basketball is a team sport. Blake needs some great teammates by his side if he wants to win a championship game. Many good players have come and gone in the three short years Blake has played for the Clippers. One example is Chauncey Billups, who left the Clippers after just two seasons. Blake Griffin, Chris Paul,

Former Clippers star Chauncey Billups left the team for the Detroit Pistons before the 2013-2014 season.

Make Connections

If an athlete supports a product, he is endorsing it. Most professional athletes earn extra money through endorsement deals. An athlete will be paid a lot of money to make a product look good. Some of the companies Blake has endorsed are Subway, Kia, and AT&T. Blake has appeared in a few television commercials and even some videogames.

and Chauncey Billups played well together, but they did not make it to the finals as the Clippers had hoped. Something else needed to be changed.

In 2013, the team decided to change direction in an even bigger way. Doc Rivers replaced the Clippers' head coach. Rivers has a lot of coaching experience. He was the coach of the Boston Celtics when they won the NBA Finals in 2008. With his help, the Clippers should be able to make it farther than they have in the past.

Just because Blake is a great player doesn't mean he can't get even better. One of his weak areas is his free-throw shots. Free throws are made from the foul line after a foul is made against a player. The player who has been fouled is the one who must make the free-throw shot. Each free throw is worth one point. Blake is known to miss these shots, which often costs his team valuable points when he is fouled.

Blake is the type of player who always works to improve himself. He can be found in the gym early every morning. He works out to improve his strength and keep himself in shape. "I don't want to be just one of the guys who just gets by or is a good player," Blake said. "I want to be one of the best and I know for a fact that you have to do all this to be one of the best." Blake will continue to get better if he keeps pushing himself hard.

PERSONAL LIFE

Blake and his brother, Taylor, are still very close. They entered the NBA draft in the same year, when the Phoenix Suns picked Taylor forty-eighth overall. Unlike Blake, Taylor did not stay with the same team, though. He spent some time in Belgium on a Belgian basketball team before returning to the United States to play for a different league. Taylor played with the Charlotte Bobcats and the Dakota Wizards. The Wizards eventually became the Santa Cruz Warriors.

Santa Cruz is in California, the same state where Blake plays. It takes about five hours to drive from Los Angeles to Santa Cruz, which means Blake and Taylor can see each other more often than they could when Taylor was in Belgium.

Blake became a father on August 1, 2013, when he had a son with Brynn Cameron. Brynn is a former basketball player for the University of South Carolina. Blake and Brynn

Blake appeared in a Subway commercial in 2012. Blake even showed up at a Los Angeles Subway restaurant to make a few sandwiches. Subway is just one of the companies Blake has worked for since joining the NBA in 2009.

Blake looks on during a free throw during a 2013 game against Detroit.

dated for a short while before breaking up. Their child is named Ford Wilson Cameron-Griffin.

Blake is very grateful for all the help his parents have given him over the years. He tries to pay them back in any way he can. He bought his parents a house and a car with some of the money he earned over the years. Blake now makes tens of millions of dollars each year, and he can easily afford these things.

Blake's first passion is basketball, but he also has a lot of other interests. He watches TV shows and movies in his free time. Some of his favorite television programs are *Modern Family, Shameless, House of Lies,* and *The Office*. He likes comedy and has said that if he weren't in the NBA, he would try to be a stand-up comedian or a writer.

Blake also enjoys travel. One of the places Blake would love to visit is Fiji. He is very adventurous and wants to try bungee jumping or skydiving one day.

Blake gave money to help people in need after a tornado ripped through town of Moore, Oklahoma. The town was almost totally destroyed and many people lost their homes in the terrible tornado. Giving to those in need is a big part of Blake's life today.

An ESPN advertisement for a game between the Los Angeles Lakers and the Clippers at the Staples Center. In the ad, Blake faces NBA star Kobe Bryant. Blake is a young player, but he's already a star to many fans.

GIVING BACK

Blake ***donates*** a lot of the money he earns to ***charity***. He started the Griffin Family Relief Fund to help families in need after the 2013 tornado in Moore, Oklahoma. The tornado was one of the largest tornados recorded in history and destroyed many homes in the area. The tragedy was very close to home for Blake and Taylor, since Moore is near Oklahoma City, where the Griffin brothers grew up. Blake donated a lot of money through the relief fund.

He has also started Project Smile Moore with his brother. Together, they visit Moore and try to bring joy to the children and families who were affected by the tornado. Anyone can donate to the relief fund through the fund's website.

Research Project

Blake Griffin donates money to charities. Using the Internet, find out more about the ways athletes help others. Make a list of different charities supported by various basketball players. Describe all the different ways basketball is helping to make the world a better place because of these players' actions.

Text-Dependent Questions

1. The author says that basketball is a "team sport." Explain what that means, and how it affects a player like Blake Griffin.

2. What is a free-throw shot?

3. According to this chapter, what is one of Blake's weaknesses?

4. What are endorsements? What has Blake endorsed?

In 2011, one of Blake Griffin's former teammates, Wilson Holloway, died of cancer. Blake wanted to honor his friend's memory after a slam-dunk contest later that year. He made headlines after one famous slam dunk where he jumped over a parked car to jam the basketball into the hoop. Blake was given the car he jumped over as a reward for winning the slam-dunk contest. He could have kept the car, but he chose to donate it to charity. The money earned through a charity auction will be used to help fund cancer research and treatment. Blake hopes that cancer research groups will be able to find a cure and help more people like his friend Wilson.

Blake has come a long, long way since the days when he was crying in daycare! Thanks to his family's love and support, he grew up to be strong man with a great deal of talent. And now, he's giving back to the world!

Series Glossary of Key Terms

All-Star Game: A game where the best players in the league form two teams and play each other.

Assist: A pass that leads to scoring points. The player who passes the ball before the other scores a basket gets the assist.

Center: A player, normally the tallest on the team, who tries to score close to the basket and defend against the other team's offense using his size.

Championship: A set of games between the two top teams in the NBA to see who is the best.

Court: The wooden or concrete surface where basketball is played. In the NBA, courts are 94 feet by 50 feet.

Defensive: Working to keep the other team from scoring points.

Draft (noun): The way NBA teams pick players from college or high school teams.

Foul: A move against another player that is against the rules, mostly involving a player touching another in a way that is not fair play.

Jump shot: A shot made from far from the basket (rather than under the basket) while the player is in the air.

Offensive: Working to score points against the other team.

Playoffs: Games at the end of the NBA season between the top teams in the league, ending in the Finals, in which the two top teams play eachother.

Point guard: The player leading the team's offense, scoring points and setting up other players to score.

Power forward: A player who can both get in close to the basket and shoot from further away. On defense, power forwards defend against both close and far shots.

Rebound: Getting the ball back after a missed shot.

Rookie: A player in his first year in the NBA.

Scouts: People who search for new basketball players in high school or college who might one day play in the NBA.

Shooting guard: A player whose job is to take shots from far away from the basket. The shooting guard is usually the team's best long-range shooter.

Small forwards: Players whose main job is to score points close to the basket, working with the other players on the team's offense.

Steal: Take the ball from a player on the other team.

Tournament: A series of games between different teams in which the winning teams move on to play other winning teams and losing teams drop out of the competition.

Find Out More

ONLINE

Griffin Family Fund
www.griffinfamilyfund.com

NBA Hoop Troop
www.nbahooptroop.com

NBA: Los Angeles Clippers
www.nba.com/clippers

Twitter: Blake Griffin
twitter.com/blakegriffin32

IN BOOKS

Frisch, Aaron. *The Story of the Los Angeles Clippers.* Mankato, Minn.: Creative Education, 2011.

Herzog, Brad. *Hoopmania: The Book of Basketball History and Trivia.* New York: Rosen, 2003.

Schaller, Bob, and Dave Harnish. *The Everything Kids' Basketball Book: The All-time Greats, Legendary Teams, Today's Superstars—and Tips on Playing like a Pro.* Avon, Mass.: Adams Media, 2009.

Stewart, Mark, and Matt Zeysing. *The Los Angeles Clippers.* Chicago: Norwood, 2009.

Wilson, Bernie. *Los Angeles Clippers.* Edina, Minn.: ABDO, 2012.

Index

About the Author

Shaina Indovino is a writer and illustrator living in Nesconset, New York. She graduated from Binghamton University, where she received degrees in sociology and English.

Picture Credits

Dreamstime.com:
- 6: Carrienelson1
- 8: Natalia Bratslavsky
- 10: Rmarmion
- 12: Zhuangmu
- 13: Eric Broder Van Dyke
- 20: Shane Link
- 24: Briancweed
- 28: Eric Broder Van Dyke
- 30: Antonio Jodice
- 32: Juan Camilo Bernal
- 38: Martin Ellis
- 40: Yaoyu Chen
- 42: MinervaStudio
- 43: Juan Camilo Bernal

Flickr.com:
- 16: Keith Allison
- 18: Bryan Horowitz
- 26: Keith Allison
- 34: Alberto Cabello
- 36: Keith Allison
- 41: LWY